In Hope
and Despair

In Hope
and Despair

Life in the Palestinian Refugee Camps

Photographs by
Mia Gröndahl

Foreword by
Hanan Ashrawi

Introduction by
Peter Hansen
United Nations Relief
and Works Agency

The American University in Cairo Press
Cairo   New York

Page ii: **Shatila Camp, Lebanon, 1999.**
Children play in a dusky alley. The refugees had
to build upward to house new generations. Now,
natural light cannot penetrate the alleys.

Page iv: **Rashidieh Camp, Lebanon, 1999.**

Pages vi-vii: **Burj el-Shemali Camp,
Lebanon, 1999.** Dalal.

page ix: **Khan Eshieh Camp, Syria, 1999.**
The children always want to know what's going on.

Copyright © 2003 by
The American University in Cairo Press
113 Sharia Kasr el Aini, Cairo, Egypt
420 Fifth Avenue, New York, NY 10018
www.aucpress.com

Photographs copyright © United Nations Relief
and Works Agency for Palestine Refugees

Dar el Kutub No. 5780/03
ISBN 977 424 811 2

Designed by
Andrea El-Akshar/AUC Press Design Center
Printed in Egypt

Contents

Foreword

By Hanan Ashrawi

IN 1948 THE PALESTINIAN PEOPLE were cast outside the course of history. Many were uprooted, displaced, and forcibly expelled from the sanctity and sanctuary of their homeland. Victims of the myth of "a land without a people for a people without a land," their narrative was suppressed, their identity denied, and their cultural and historical realities distorted.

For more than half a century, the Palestinians have been subjected to the dual injustice of dispossession, dispersal, and exile on the one hand and the oppression of a brutal military occupation, a denial of their basic human rights, and a systematic policy of oppression on the other.

This year, as we painfully mark the 55th anniversary of al-Nakba ('the Catastrophe'), we are reminded of the continued suffering of more than five million Palestinian refugees worldwide, who constitute the majority of the Palestinian people, and are unquestionably the living embodiment of the Palestinians' tragic plight and their quest for justice.

In the occupied Palestinian territories, Jordan, Syria, and Lebanon, al-Mukhayyam ('the Camp') has become both a symbol of Palestinian perseverance and determination and a reminder of Palestinian suffering. While Palestinian refugees in the camps seek to preserve their identity and nourish their longing to return home one day, they continue to languish under extreme conditions of poverty, deprivation, fear, and uncertainty. Still they have never lost sight of their essential humanity.

Israel's repeated denial of the legitimate right of the Palestinian refugees to return to their homes is a negation of the Palestinian narrative itself and a perpetuation of al-Nakba in different ways and forms. United Nations Resolution 194, the legal framework of the Palestinian refugees' right of return, is tantamount to the international community's obligation and commitment to end the grave historical injustices inflicted on the Palestinian refugee population.

Fifty-five years after al-Nakba, the fourth

generation of Palestinian refugees is born stateless and automatically uprooted amid the ruins of al-Mukhayyam. Whole Palestinian families of different generations continue to bear the scars of a nation betrayed, its very humanity denied. Yet rather than becoming objects of pity, they are symbols of determination, hope, and a commitment to life.

The images captured by Mia Gröndahl for this vital initiative are a moving testimony to this dual reality of the Palestinian refugees and an indispensable witness to the triumph of the human spirit over perpetual pain.

To look beyond the abstraction of Palestinians as numbers and faceless victims, to reach out to capture the human essence of the Palestinian narrative, is an important contribution to the liberation of the Palestinian people and the restoration of their rights. By capturing instant moments in the lives of Palestinian refugees, Mia Gröndahl has compressed both time and space to generate a most powerful tool of constructive perception and human identification.

Thus the lens of her camera has visually depicted the collective memory of the Palestinians as a powerful force for human affirmation while simultaneously creating a moving tribute to individual courage.

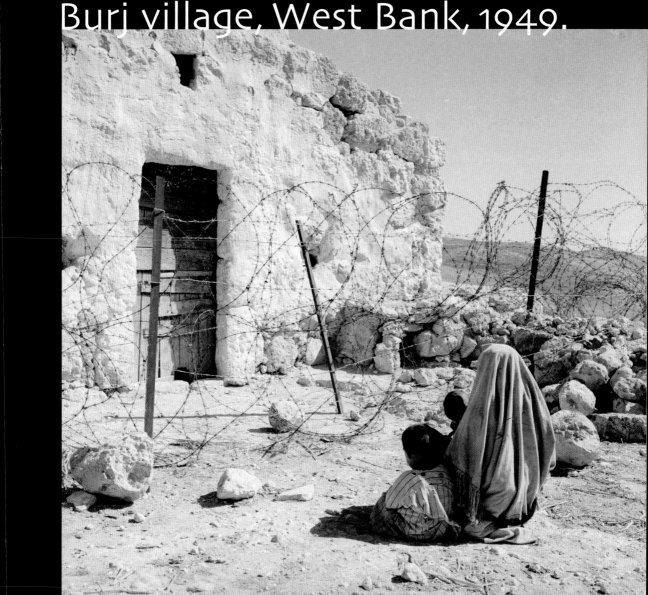

Burj village, West Bank, 1949.

Jaffa, 1948.

Last hours in Jaffa. Barefoot and pushing their belongings in prams and carts, Palestinian families leave the Mediterranean coastal town that became part of the greater Tel Aviv area, Israel. UN photo, 1948.

Jalazone Camp, West Bank, 1951.

Nahr el-Bared Camp, Lebanon, 1951

During the first years the refugees of 1948
lived in tented camps. Nahr el-Bared in
northern Lebanon was one of the first
refugee camps set up to provide shelter for
the hundreds of thousands of Palestinians
who lost their homes, lands, and livelihoods
after the 1948 Arab–Israeli war. UNRWA
photo by Jack Madvo, 1951.

Allenby Bridge, June 1967.

The Palestinians were again forced to flee in 1967, carrying the sick, the old, and the frail and their few belongings on their backs, across the demolished bridge into Jordan. The land behind them fell under Israeli

Baqa'a Camp, Jordan, 1975.

Introduction

By Peter Hansen

UNRWA BELIEVES PHOTOGRAPHY is an important element in telling the story of the Palestine refugees. This is something that we have always believed at the United Nations Relief and Works Agency for Palestine Refugees (UNRWA), and it shows. The Agency has taken it upon itself to maintain an unequaled photographic record of the lives and history of those in its care. This documentary record now runs to over 30,000 still images in black-and-white and color. In addition, UNRWA has hundreds of hours of film footage; raw and edited, spanning four decades and many generations of refugee experience.

The UN General Assembly created UNRWA in 1949 with a simple mandate to ease the conditions of starvation and distress of the more than 700,000 refugees forced to flee from the 1948 Arab–Israeli War. Since then, UNRWA's mandate has evolved, so that its longstanding commitment to the Palestinians is unique in the annals of humanitarian relief. The Agency's education, health care, and social programs amount to an extended investment in the human development of the refugees and their descendants. There are now four million refugees registered with the Agency across Lebanon, Syria, Jordan, the West Bank, and the Gaza Strip. The Agency provides assistance that ranges from skills training for youth and shelter rehabilitation for the very poor to emergency food aid for the 1.1 million refugees made destitute by the conflict in the occupied Palestinian territory that broke out in September 2000.

UNRWA's investment in the refugees is funded solely by voluntary contributions from the international community, and therefore the Agency must work hard to keep the story of the refugees alive. In the pre–mass media age of the early 1950s, when the Agency was young, it was not inevitable that UNRWA would put so much energy into the creation of a comprehensive visual record. It was primarily thanks to the efforts of one British photographer, Myrtle Winter Chaumeny, that the Agency began to take photography so seriously.

Maintaining hygiene under very basic conditions. UNRWA photo by George Nehmeh, 1975.

Winter Chaumeny, who headed UNRWA's audio-visual section from the early 1950s until her retirement in 1978, was instrumental in fostering a culture where generations of photographers were able to combine visual flair and artistry with the need to publicize and document the plight of the Palestinian dispossessed. Whether Palestinian or international, freelancers or staff members, talented photographers have been held in especially high regard by UNRWA.

Mia Gröndahl's work for the Agency, which comprises the bulk of this book, is just the latest expression of that esteem. Her work has brought a fresh collection of images, full of color, compassion, and humanity, into the UNRWA archive. Gröndahl's photographs are much more than a simple record of poverty, overcrowding, and despair to be used to encourage donations. They also bring the viewer unexpected humor and flashes of pure beauty. They stand proudly with the classics in UNRWA's archive by photographers such as Jack Madvo, George Nehmeh, and Myrtle Winter Chaumeny.

Much of the work of UNRWA, from medical care to education, has had a lasting impact on the lives of the Palestine refugees. Just as lasting is the incredible photographic record, of which this book is part, that has been made possible by the Agency's longstanding appreciation of the power of the visual image. Every people needs a history, and in recording the lives of the refugees over five decades UNRWA has in its own small way contributed to maintaining the identity of the Palestinian people for future generations. It is because of this that the United Nations hopes that UNRWA's photographic archive, including the images in this book, will one day become the property of the Palestinian people themselves.

Life in the Palestinian Refugee Camps

By Mia Gröndahl

IT TOOK A LONG TIME before the world saw the Palestinian refugees. If nobody sees you in this world, it is almost as if you do not exist. "Where were you?" the old Palestinian woman asked me with anger in her voice. "Where were you in 1948 when I had to flee without any shoes on my feet from my village? And where were you when I was uprooted a second time in 1967?" She had been living for almost fifty years in a poor shelter in a refugee camp in Jordan.

The western media instead had their focus on the victors, the colonialists and immigrants who in the end managed to take over Palestine and turn it into Israel. While the success story of the Israeli 'pioneers' was spread all over the world, the Palestinian people were to a large degree made invisible. If we do not see people, if nothing is written about them, we do not get to know them. A faceless crowd will never receive our understanding, even less our sympathy.

As I grew up, the world sympathized with the Israelis. The shadow of the Holocaust was still hanging over Europe and we, the genera-tion born after the war, were raised in the belief that the Israelis were still victims. I, like many young Scandinavians, traveled to "the young and vibrant state," as the propaganda described the country, to live and work for a couple of months on a kibbutz. Many years later I learned that the kibbutz of Ma'agan Mikha'el was built in 1950 on land that belonged to the Palestinian village of Kabara, which was one of the almost 500 Palestinian villages destroyed by the Jewish forces in 1948–49. Its 120 inhabitants were among the nearly one million Palestinians who were forced to flee their homes and seek refuge in neighboring countries.

The one million Palestinian refugees from 1948 have today become more than 4 million people. Many of them live under very difficult conditions in overcrowded camps in Lebanon, Jordan, Syria, the West Bank, and Gaza, the lat-ter territories still occupied by Israel. On my first visit in a refugee camp, I felt my eyes were almost overpowered by the chaos of concrete shelters, corrugated metal roofs held in place with more rough concrete blocks, a muddle of electrical wires crossing the air, and narrow alleys with open sewage channels running along the middle. It was a chaos painted in ugly shades of gray. No trees, plants, or flowers could be seen. Wherever I pointed my camera lens, I felt my sense of natural harmony disturbed to such a degree that I did not know how to capture what appeared in front of my eyes.

Still, I found an abundance of beauty in the camps. It belonged to the people. I found it in their faces and the way they carried themselves: a proud yet friendly stature. I still wonder from where the refugees are drawing their friendliness, hospitality, and willingness to open their hearts and houses to my camera and all my questions about their lives, the past, the present, and their hopes and dreams for the future. I traveled from camp to camp across the borders of the Middle East, and everywhere I went I was received with the same warm "Ahlan wa sahlan"— "We welcome you as a member of our family."

I met people I will never forget. I will always remember the two old sisters Fatma and Hamda. From their mud hut in the Jordan Valley they can see their old homeland on the other side of the river. The sisters, who became refugees in 1948, sat in the opening to their poor one-room shelter and described their village, Umm 'Ajra, in detail—every house and alley, all the plants that grew in the fields. I realized from the way they talked that they did not know that nothing was left of their village today, that all the houses have been leveled to the ground, and that an Israeli settlement has taken over the land.

I also often think of Mahmoud Zigari and the key he still keeps to his old house. Eighty-year-old Mahmoud lives in a refugee camp on the outskirts of Bethlehem. Zakhariya, the village where he was born and grew up, is only a couple of kilometers from the camp. Every Friday. Mahmoud breaks the occupier's law and crosses the border to Israel, where he climbs the hills with the big iron key in his pocket to pray in the ruins of his old home.

And I will never forget Badr and her immense love for her nine children. The family lived in a barren two-room shelter in a refugee camp in Lebanon. There was no furniture, only a pile of thin mattresses to be laid out on the cold concrete floor in the evening and an old black-and-white television. Badr told me about her dream of being able to give all her children a good education. But even more important to her was that her children grow up to be real human beings—people who are kind to others.

When I look at the photographs I took of Fatma, Hamda, Mahmoud, Badr, and all the other people I met in the refugee camps, I think of them as my family—they could have been my mother, father, aunt, sister, or brother, and the children could have been my children. Look into their eyes, and you will meet people who deserve not only our sympathy and understanding, but also our voice to help them fulfill their right of return to their homeland.

Burj el-Barajneh Camp, Lebanon, 1999. "If I were a pigeon," says the boy, "I would fly to our home village in Palestine."

Shatila Camp, Lebanon, 1999. The only open area by the camp is the garbage dump.

Beddawi Camp, Lebanon, 1999.
Playing in the small open-air storage
area behind the family's kitchen.

Burj el-Barajneh, Lebanon, 1999. Every camp
alley is overrun by children of all ages. More than half of
the population of the camps is under the age of fifteen.

Beddawi Camp, Lebanon, 1999. Trying to make contact with the life in the alley that she is not allowed to enter—this girl's parents were psychologically scarred by the civil war and do not feel secure anywhere except inside their rundown shelter, where they keep a close watch over their seven children.

Shatila Camp, Lebanon, 1999. The only window that brings some daylight to the Ajina family's dark shelter.

Beddawi Camp, Lebanon, 1999. Sama' is six years old.

Left: **Burj el-Barajneh Camp, Lebanon, 1999.** Suddenly his shyness takes over and he doesn't dare to look at me anymore; but he still smiles.

Burj el-Shemali Camp, Lebanon,
1999. Shireen hides from her playmates
in the backyard of her family's shelter.

Beddawi Camp, Lebanon, 1999.
In the protective arms of an older brother.

Rashidieh Camp, Lebanon, 1999.

Shatila Camp, Lebanon, 1999.

Following pages:
Rashidieh Camp, Lebanon, 1999.
The sea is a wonderful playground.

Beddawi Camp, Lebanon, 1999.
The silent girl who never stops petting her rabbit.

Nahr al-Bared, Lebanon, 1999. Many people keep pigeons on the rooftops. The birds are a supplemental food source and some are also used as carrier pigeons.

Nahr el-Bared Camp, Lebanon, 1999.

Nahr el-Bared Camp, Lebanon, 1999. The only palm grove in the camp is the one painted on the wall, on which hang portraits of the family's deceased men; one of them is Samiha's husband, who left her alone with eight children.

Right:
Nahr el-Bared Camp, Lebanon, 1999. Hyam (far left) and her children visit the grave of her husband, who died a year ago at the age of thirty. Hyam has planted her husband's favorite plant, the geranium, on his resting place.

Wavell Camp, Lebanon, 1999. Nami with Muhammad, the youngest of her three children. Sometimes Nami, who is a widow, finds work as a cleaner in nearby Baalbek; otherwise, she and her children are totally dependent on food rations from UNRWA.

Wavell Camp, Lebanon, 1999. Muhammad watches television, a window to a world so different from the life of the camp that it could be another planet.

Right:
Rashidieh Camp, Lebanon, 1999. Khaldiya has given birth seven times, and the only child to survive delivery was Muhammad. In three months she is expecting her eighth child.

Beddawi Camp, Lebanon, 1999. Majda Khalil's seven children are her pride and joy—everyone is healthy. Now and then her husband finds work in a country where Palestinians are barred from participating in over seventy-five trades and professions.

Beddawi Camp, Lebanon, 1999. Majda lifts her youngest child, a five-month-old baby, from the hanging cradle.

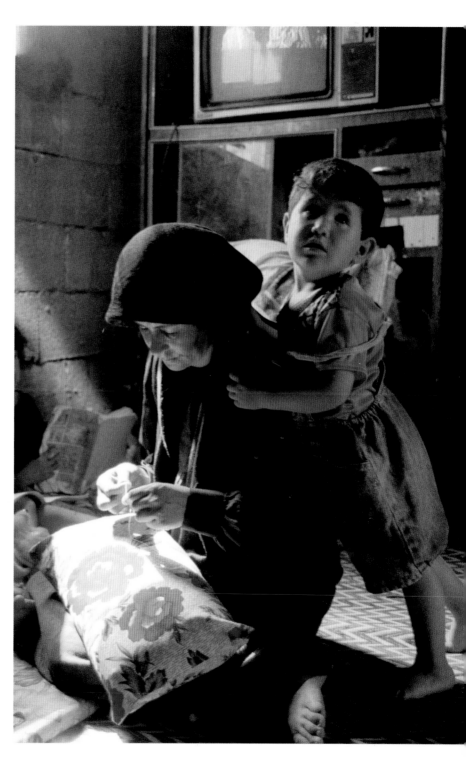

Nahr el-Bared Camp, Lebanon, 1999. Badr, mother of nine, has finally found a moment to mend some of her children's clothes.

Nahr el-Bared Camp,
Lebanon, 1999. Badr's
kitchen is in the small court-
yard outside the family's
corrugated iron shelter.

Nahr el-Bared Camp, Lebanon, 1999. "He is intelligent.
I can see it in his eyes!" says Badr, who dreams of being able to
give her youngest son, Ibrahim, a good education. But even more
important to Badr is that all her children grow up to be real human
beings—people who are kind to others.

Beddawi Camp, Lebanon, 1999. Miriam al-Saleh supports her large
family working as a maid and cleaner in the wealthy homes of nearby Tripoli.
Her husband suffers from asthma and cannot ease her burden. In summer
some of the children sleep in the open court to give more space to the rest
of the family in their tiny two-room shelter.

Beddawi Camp, Lebanon, 1999. When Nadia Shahin's husband, Adnan, woke up from a long coma, he was totally paralyzed from his neck to his feet and had lost his ability to speak. Nadia takes care of Adnan, who now has his sickbed in the living room, while she sleeps here alone.

Burj el-Shemali Camp, Lebanon, 1999. Dalal, twenty-one years old, with her youngest sister, Reem. The family lives in two small rooms, with mattresses as the only furniture.

Left:
Beddawi Camp, Lebanon, 1999. Tahara lives with her seven children, the youngest a week-old baby, in a ground-floor shelter that is in darkness most of the day.

Beddawi Camp, Lebanon, 1999. No one could remember when the bird in the cage stopped singing.

Following pages:
Burj el-Shemali Camp, Lebanon, 1999. From the one tap on the tank, Hanan washes herself and fills huge plastic basins to wash the dishes and the clothes for her family of twelve.

Latakia Camp, Syria, 1999.
Happy to be the center of attention at
the women's center during a training
course for future hairdressers.

Beddawi Camp, Lebanon, 1999.
A young girl brushes her hair.

Latakia Camp, Syria, 1999. Muna and her friends never miss Monday's aerobics class.

Burj al-Barajneh, Lebanon, 1999.
Every millimeter of the crowded camp must be used.

Rashidieh Camp, Lebanon, 1999.
Hanaa has a brand new sink in her small kitchen.

Beddawi Camp, Lebanon, 1999.
A boy carries an armful of newly harvested mulukhiya. The leaves are stripped from the stalks and used to make a classic Middle Eastern soup.

Burj el-Barajneh Camp, Lebanon, 1999. The spinach season.

Wavell Camp, Lebanon, 1999.
A sack of flour must last for the next
three months.

Wavell Camp, Lebanon, 1999.
A busy morning at the UNRWA food
distribution center.

Khan Eshieh, Syria.
Every morning the women
collect their water from a
tank brought to the camp
by UNRWA.

**Amman New Camp,
Jordan, 2000.** Today,
UNRWA provides food rations
to over 200,000 refugees who
are registered in the special
hardship program.

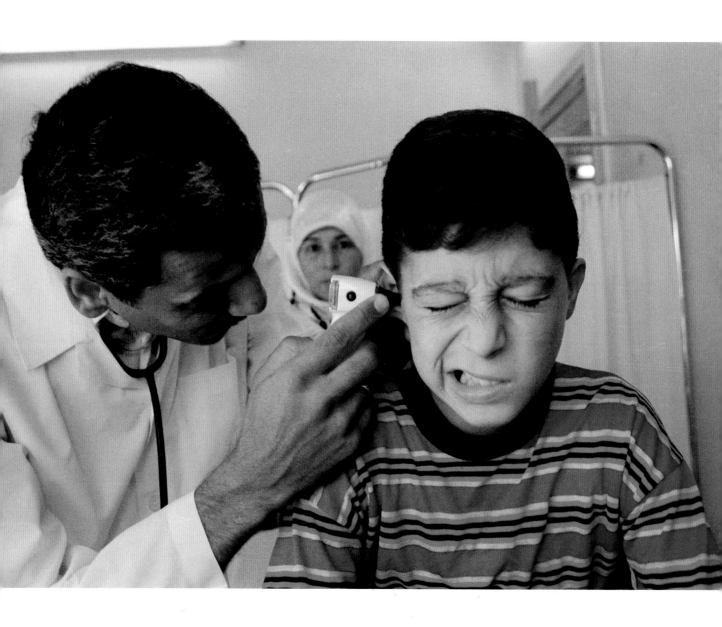

Dummar Health Center,
Damascus, Syria, 1999.
On average, each UNRWA doctor
sees a hundred patients a day.

Bureij Camp, Gaza Strip,
1999. Khaled's family has just
brought home their food rations.

Beddawi Camp, Lebanon, 1999.
Another morning.

Beddawi Camp, Lebanon, 1999. Mother Saada and her son Younis, who suffers from rheumatism, have lived in the same shelter since 1953. Saada fled her village, al-Buwayziya, in May 1948, when it became known that the nearby city of Safed had fallen to the Israeli forces.

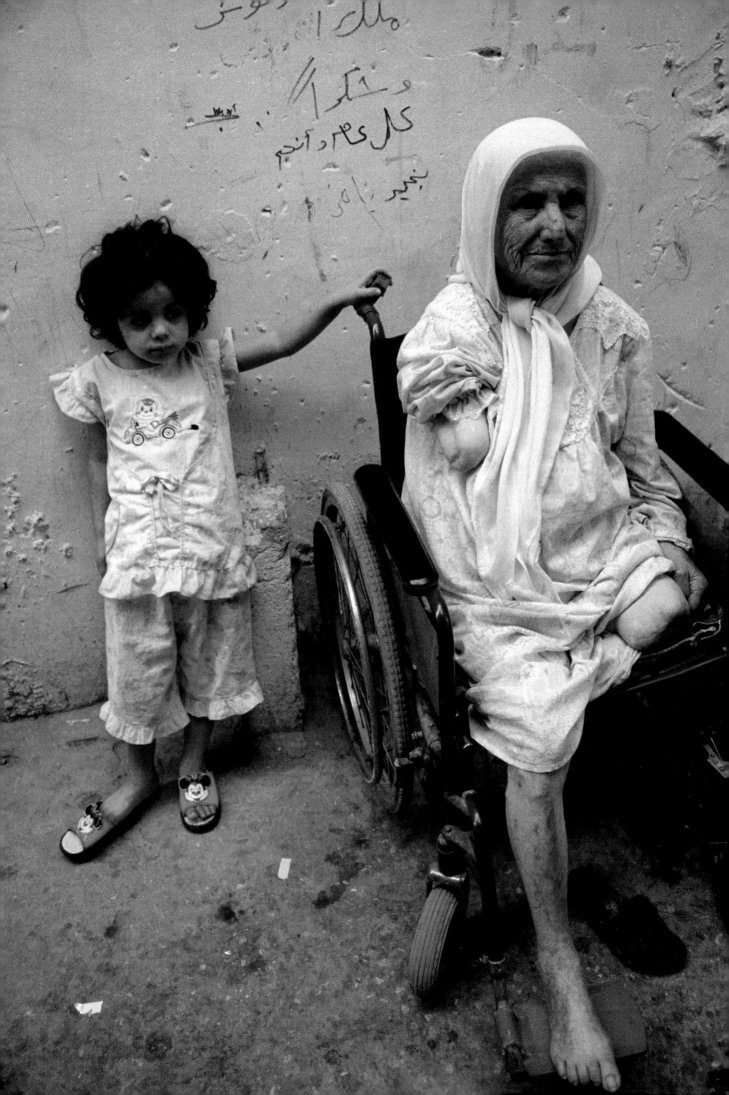

Burj el-Barajneh Camp, Lebanon, 1999. Yasmine Atout,
eighty years old, with her granddaughter. Yasmine lost her right arm
and left leg when her shelter was bombed during the hostilities in
Lebanon. She has not moved from the alley in the camp for the last
eighteen years because her wheelchair is broken and she cannot
afford to repair it. The writing on the wall says: "Have a nice year!"

Burj el-Barajneh
Camp, Lebanon,
1999. The general store.

Khan Eshieh Camp, Syria, 1999. "This is no life.
I wish I had died in 1948 instead of turning generations
and generations of my family into refugees," says Abu
Hassan (right), eighty-three years old, sitting with his
son. They have been barred by Israel from returning to
their home village of Shafa Amr, near the city of Haifa,
for more than fifty years.

Nahr el-Bared Camp,
Lebanon, 1999.
Hassan al-Jamal was once
a freedom fighter.

Beddawi Camp, Lebanon, 1999.
Palestine, the old homeland, hangs as a
piece of jewelry around Talal Ajou's neck.

Beddawi Camp, Lebanon, 1999. Manar Ajou's son,
17-year-old Talal, is the best in his class and wants to become
a doctor. They worry about how they will pay for his studies.

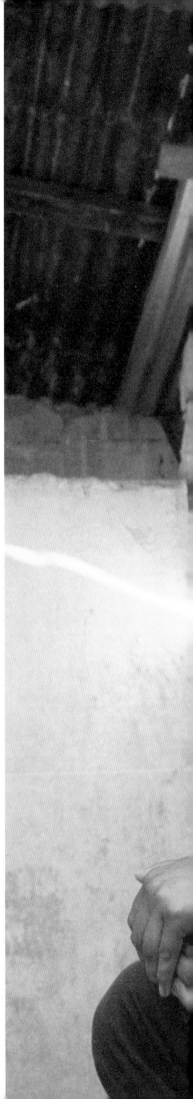

Burj el-Shemali Camp, Lebanon, 1999.
Hanan has graduated from school with excellent
grades and won a place at Siblin Vocational
Training Center, run by UNRWA. She is trying to
study her way out of the camp.

Baqa'a Camp, Jordan, 1999.
Teenagers in the camp.

Following pages:
Husn Camp, Jordan, 1999.

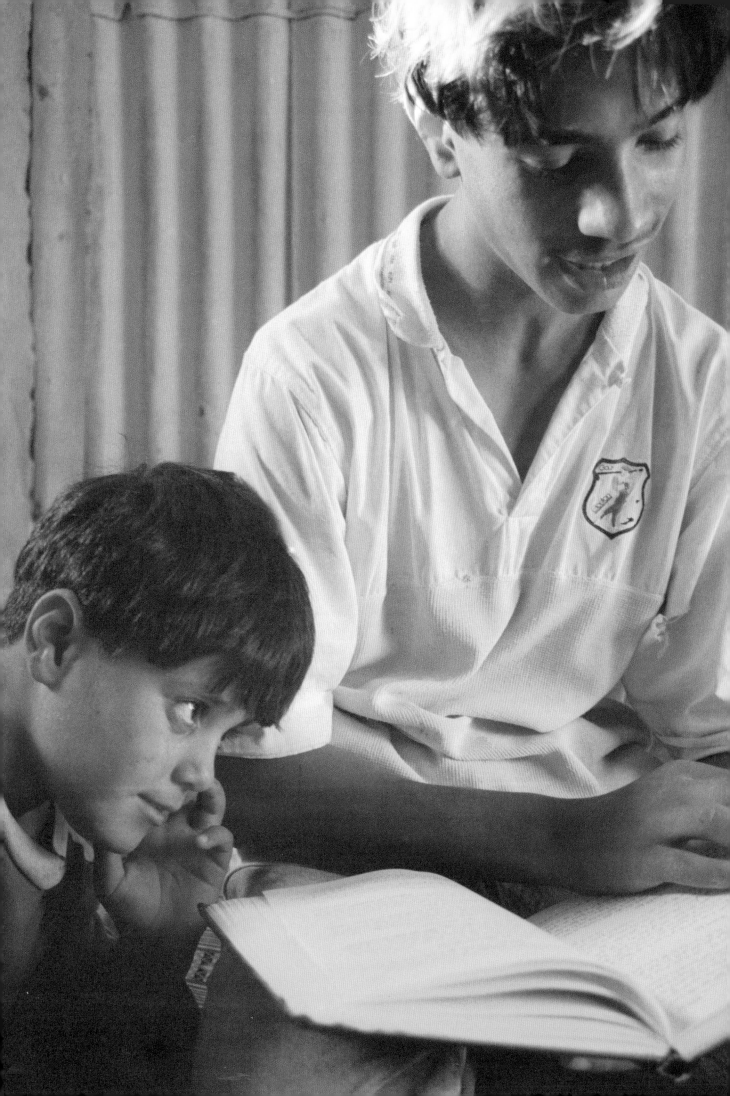

Husn Camp, Jordan,
1999. Sister and brother on
a street in the camp.

Husn Camp, Jordan,
1999. The road to the camp.

Left:
Husn Camp, Jordan,
1999. Mahmoud listens to
his brother Ahmed reading.

Jerash Camp, Jordan, 1999. In the shelter where Nahil Nabeh Rantissi lives with her six children, one of the girls wants to show off her chickens. Suddenly the shelter is turned into a chaos of flapping wings and happy children running around chasing the birds.

Jerash Camp, Jordan, 1999. After the chase.

Jerash Camp, Jordan, 2000.
A boy on the way to the camp's
oven to bake his mother's bread.

Baqa'a Camp, Jordan, 2000.
Two friends at the market.

Amman New Camp, Jordan,
2000. Laughing in the rain.

Talbieh Camp, Jordan, 2000.
Most of the time their parents can't
afford the kerosene for the stove.

Baqa'a Camp, Jordan, 2000.
Heavy winter rains have turned the
road into a river of mud.

Jerash Camp, Jordan, 2000.
Muhammad in the winter rain.

Jerash Camp, Jordan, 2000.
A Middle Eastern winter can be
bitterly cold.

Sukhneh Camp, Jordan, 2000. Omar Musa
and his sisters, Huda and Waed, are responsible for
five goats and two donkeys. The animals and a small
income from an older brother support their ten-
member family, all of whom share the same room.

Sukhneh Camp, Jordan,
2000. Waed, aged six, outside
the family's one-room shelter.

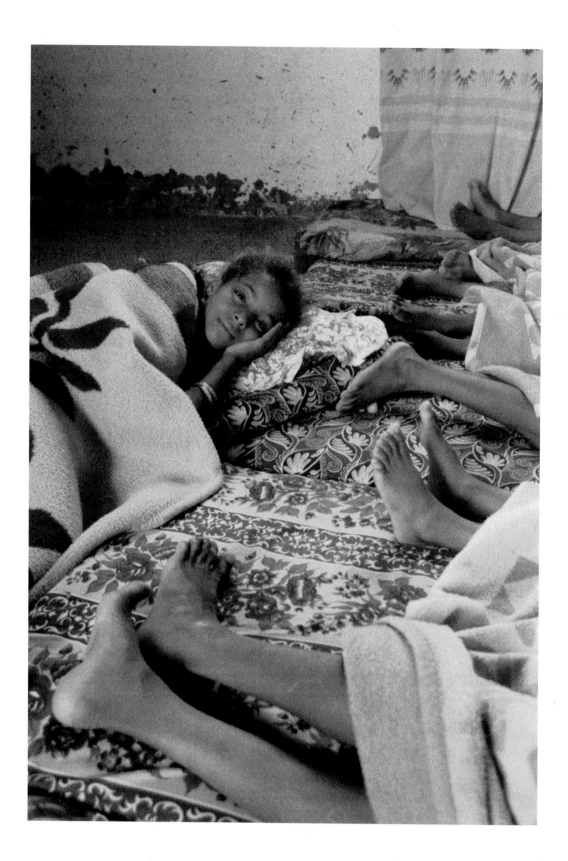

In Hope and Despair

Baqa'a Camp, Jordan, 1999.
When it's time to go to sleep, the
Ibrahim family, who live in two
rooms and a kitchen, put down thin
mattresses on the floor.

Left:
Husn Camp, Jordan, 1999. Samah picks corn in her family's tiny garden. There is a narrow strip along the border of the camp where the refugees can grow vegetables.

Husn Camp, Jordan, 1999.

Husn Camp, Jordan, 2000. Samah seldom leaves the kitchen. Her mother is dead and her father fears the day when she will marry, leaving nobody to take care of him and the thirteen younger children.

Following pages:
Jerash Camp, Jordan, 1999. Since her son-in-law lost both his legs, Nasra, the pillar of the family, takes care of her daughter and her five grandchildren.

Jordan Valley, Jordan, 1999. Fatma Agil tries her best to take care of herself and her sister Hamda, who can no longer walk. Both in their eighties, they have no relatives able to look after them. From their mud hut, they can see their home town, Baysan, in the distance. Fatma and Hamda, who became refugees in 1948, can describe their village, Umm 'Ajra, and nearby Baysan in detail—every house and alley, and all the plants that grew in the fields. They don't know that nothing is left of the village today and that its lands belong to an Israeli settlement.

Jerash Camp, Jordan, 1999. Amina still wears the traditional Palestinian embroidered dress from her home village.

Souf Camp, Jordan,
2000. Wahiba, ninety years
old, lives alone in a corrugated
iron shelter without electricity
or running water.

Jerash Camp, Jordan, 1999. During the British Mandate, Ibrahim Hamoudi Sirri, now aged seventy-six, served as a soldier in Jaffa, his hometown. In 1948, Ibrahim and his family had to flee to Gaza, and in 1967, when Israel occupied the Gaza Strip, the family was uprooted a second time. Ibrahim now shares his simple shelter with a brother.

Sukhneh Camp, Jordan, 2000. Waiting for customers to buy wool, Awad Mohawish is a refugee from Beersheba, one of several cities that was entirely emptied of their Palestinian inhabitants in 1948.

Madaba Camp, Jordan, 2000.
The children stand with cold hands and feet around Mutawa Muhammad Hafi, eighty-five years old, who proudly declares: "I'm from Hatta village in Palestine."

Beach Camp, Gaza Strip, 2002.

Husn Camp, Jordan, 1999. A man proudly wears his red and white keffiyeh.

Camp No. 1, West Bank, 1999. The
children make way for the old man in a hurry.

Beach Camp, Gaza Strip, 2002.
Graffiti by the sea.

Left:
Beach Camp, Gaza Strip, 2002.
A refugee shelter from the early 1950s.

Following pages:
Beach Camp, Gaza Strip, 1999.
Kings of the new asphalt road.

Beach Camp, Gaza Strip, 2002.
Muhammad accompanies his father to
ask for extra food rations at the UNRWA
distribution center.

Beach Camp, Gaza Strip, 1999. Two sisters.

Beach Camp, Gaza Strip,
2002. The grandchildren of
Abu Sultan.

Right:
Deir el-Balah Camp,
Gaza Strip, 2000.

Right:
Maghazi Camp, Gaza Strip, 2000.
Farrah Abu Aish has given birth to fourteen children.

Maghazi Camp, Gaza Strip, 2000.
Farrah prepares tea in her tiny kitchen.

Maghazi Camp, Gaza Strip, 2000.
The shelter's open-air bathroom.

Maghazi Camp, Gaza Strip, 2000.
Farah's little son.

Khan Younis Camp, Gaza
Strip, 2000. This boy is one of
48 employees in a workshop that
produces overalls for Israeli clothing
companies.

Left:
Jalazone Camp, West Bank,
1999. A child plays on the garbage
dump—environmental conditions still
remain appalling in many of the camps.

Following pages:
Left:
Maghazi Camp, Gaza
Strip, 1999. An open channel
of sewage flows down the alley.

Right:
Nuseirat Camp, Gaza
Strip, 1999. Jumping over a
dangerous snake of sewage.

Wadi Gaza, Gaza Strip, 2000. Bedouin refugee
women take care of the sheep and the goats, while the
men tend to the camels.

Wadi Gaza, Gaza Strip, 2000. A Bedouin woman in front of her family's makeshift encampment. The Bedouin in the wadi are refugees expelled from the Beersheba district.

Following pages:
Khan Younis, Gaza Strip, 2001. Salem Abu Musa laments the destruction of his home by the Israeli army, which has left his family of sixteen homeless.

Rafah, Gaza Strip,
2001. Khalil Ghassan
Abu Libde lost both his
house and his leg in an
Israeli incursion.

Khan Younis Camp,
Gaza Strip, 2002.
A boy collects fragments
of the ceramic tiles that
used to cover the floors
of his house.

Shu'fat Camp, West Bank, 2000. Located north of
Jerusalem, the camp needs more space for its 1,200 inhabitants,
but the surrounding land is occupied by Israel. The light shines
on the Israeli settlement across the valley.

Aqabat Jabr Camp,
West Bank, 1999.

Following pages:
Jenin Camp, West Bank, 2002. Two-year-old
Hussein was separated from his family for three weeks,
lost in the chaos when the Israeli army invaded the camp.
No one knew that he had been taken care of by a
neighbor who managed to escape the occupying forces
and seek refuge in a Palestinian village outside the camp.

Nablus, West Bank, April 2002.
Hours after the three-week siege is lifted
and the tanks have pulled out from the city
center, seventy people killed during the Israeli
incursion are hastily buried in the same grave.

Jenin Camp, West Bank, 2002. When the Israeli tanks pulled out from the camp,
the residents returned to their leveled homes in the hope of finding something salvageable.

Jenin Camp, West Bank, 2002. Three weeks ago this
little girl lived here, played with her friends and called it home.

Jenin Camp, West Bank, 2002. A plastic
plant has survived the work of the Israeli bulldozers.

Camp No. 1, West Bank,
1999. A woman crouches in
one of the narrow, dark alleys
of the camp.

Jenin Camp, West Bank,
2002. Carrying what is left of
their belongings on their backs,
two brothers leave the ruins of
the camp, destroyed by Israel's
'Operation Defensive Shield.'

Jalazone Camp, West Bank, 2000.
The coffeeshop is a meeting place during the
day for the camp's elderly men.

Dheisheh Camp, West Bank, 1998.
Mahmoud Zigari with the key to his old house. Every
Friday he breaks the occupier's law and crosses the
border into Israel to walk up the hill to the destroyed
village where he was born and grew up, and from which
he was forced to flee in April 1948.

Following pages:
Dheisheh Camp, West Bank, 1999. Manar Faraj
prepares herself for a performance of the Ibdaa dance
troupe. In Arabic, *ibdaa* means 'to create something out
of nothing.' The young refugees in the Ibdaa dance troupe
use their performance to express the history, struggle, and
aspirations of the Palestinian people—specifically, the right
to return to their homeland.

**Burj el-Shemali Camp,
Lebanon, 1999.** Basma has been
a refugee for fifty-five years; her
hope for return to her home village
in northern Palestine never died.

Tulkarm Camp, West Bank, 1999. Education has always been seen as the refugees' hope for a better future. Today, there are over 458,000 refugee children registered in the UNRWA schools.

Tulkarm Camp, West Bank, 1999. Enthusiasm reigns at an UNRWA girls' school. All Palestinian refugee children are entitled to free basic elementary and preparatory schooling for up to ten years.

Tulkarm Camp, West Bank, 1999. Overcrowded classrooms are common and UNRWA is forced to run most of its schools on double shifts.

Right:
Tulkarm Camp, West Bank, 1999. The happiness of experiencing the world upside-down—a physical education class in an UNRWA girls' school.

Tulkarm Camp, West Bank, 1999.
The first one to the end of the road is the winner.